# THE BUDGETING BOOK FOR YOUNG ADULTS

---

## GUIDE ON BUDGETING BASICS FOR BEGINNERS, INCLUDING THE 50/30/20 BUDGET

**Sasha Winters**

SASHA WINTERS

ISBN
978-1-387-88604-3

# TABLE OF CONTENTS

SASHA WINTERS

# SPECIAL BONUS!

Get this **50/30/20 Budget Template**, which is a pre-formatted template complete with formulas and sample budget items, 100% FREE!

| 50 / 30 / 20 Budget | | | | |
| --- | --- | --- | --- | --- |
| **Monthly sources of income** | **Sources** | **Monthly Amount** | | |
| | Source 1 | $ 4,000.00 | | |
| | Source 2 | $ - | | |
| | Source 3 | $ - | | |
| | Source 4 | $ - | | |
| *Total Take-home Income* | | $ 4,000.00 | | |
| **50/30/20 Allocations** | **Needs (50%)** | | **Wants (30%)** | **Savings (20%)** |
| Total for category | $ 2,000.00 | | $ 1,200.00 | $ 800.00 |

Hundreds of others are already enjoying insider access to all of my current and future books, 100% free! If you want insider access plus this the **50/30/20 Budget Template,** all you have to do is **scan the code below** with your smartphone camera to claim your offer!

SASHA WINTERS

# CHAPTER ONE

## INTRODUCTION

---

Money is something we can't get enough of. It is fair to say that our lives' quality depends on our ability to manage and control our money. So, if you don't feel as if you have the right tools for money management, learning about budgeting is a great place to start. You can dramatically improve your life quality, live out your dreams, and plan for your future without feeling insecure and afraid about your finances. Using this book, you can take simple steps to bring your finances under control and keep them there.

Regardless of how much you earn, you can be more financially secure within the limits of your resources. However, to effectively plan and manage your money, you need to have a budget document. A budget is simply a plan for allocating your money according to your needs and wants. With a solid budget that you design yourself, you'll be able to meet both needs and wants as well as secure your future.

Living on a budget only implies that your money spent is well planned, not that you won't get what you need. Simply, a budget is a summary of plans for how to meet spending goals. A budget puts your income side by side with your expenses. Since income and expenses can vary and come due at irregular intervals, a budget helps you understand timing and allocate accordingly. Also, your plans and funding should be reviewed frequently.

Many books are written on the subject because people find that they live much better when income and expenses are clear and under control. This book will provide useful and easy-to-use tools to help anyone have a clearer picture of their finances and gain more power in that area.

**Where to start?**

We all have many competing needs and wants. Without a complete and comprehensive view of what we make and where it goes, it's easy for a personal or family budget to get seriously off track. Typically, we need money to pay off debts, keep up with day-to-day living expenses, save for rainy days, and for retirement. That may seem pretty daunting, but with this book and a 50/30/20 budget plan, you will be ready to take on that challenge. The reason I wrote this book is to enable people to use a simple but powerful budgeting process to build a balanced framework and approach that ensures that needs, wants, and savings all get appropriate attention in the monthly budget—resulting in better outcomes and greater peace of mind. This book will outline the easy steps you can take. You won't need more than a paper and a calculator to get right to the heart of your finances and start making improvements.

First popularized by Elizabeth Warren, a US Senator and presidential candidate, the 50/30/20 budget rule helps by allocating specific budget percentages to needs, wants, and savings, helping even budgeting beginners get off to a great start with their finances. For recent college graduates and others first entering the workforce and beginning to manage their own money, a 50/30/20 can help set up long-term success. For those who have been managing money for a while, it provides a sanity check against current spending habits. It helps give a quick assessment of whether you are on track toward your financial goals or not.

The rule states that 50% of your income after tax should go toward actual needs, 30% should go toward wants, while the remaining 20% should be saved or used to pay off debts. Saving for the future can mean anything from buying a laptop or a house to funding retirement.

Most financial experts believe that one's needs should not include more than these five subcategories, namely: housing, food, transportation, clothing, insurance premiums, and miscellaneous (which includes day-to-day utilities). For wants, the subcategories include things like education, entertainment, vacations, and benevolence. The savings category includes necessary debt payments, emergency fund savings, large purchase savings, and retirement savings. By applying the 50/30/20 rule to your overall expense picture, you will be able to balance finances to meet your and your family's needs.

The hardest part of budgeting is probably the saving part. If a person doesn't set savings goals and targets, it's very easy to spend money simply because it's available. With a budget that prioritizes savings, you have an opportunity to be more thoughtful about purchases.

Let's get started.

## IMPORTANCE OF PLANNING AND BUDGETING

Achieving a well-balanced budget with substantial savings has so many positive aspects, including:

- Avoiding interest: It is essential to understand the effect of interest on the costs of your purchases. Buying on credit just means that you are borrowing from your future to pay for the present, and you actually pay more for purchases when you pay interest on them.

- Facing emergencies: It is essential to have savings to live with some confidence level, enabling you to enjoy life without worrying too much about emergency expenses. You'll sleep better knowing you have put plans in place for a secure future.

- Better life decisions: Budgeting makes it easier to decide everything from jobs, to where to live, to significant purchases.

- Taking a pulse on hobbies: You'll also know if any of your hobbies or habits are throwing off your future plans.

- Understanding where the money goes: Tracking even the smallest expenses helps create a more transparent financial picture. One seemingly insignificant daily spending habit can actually add up to a significant amount over a month's time. Budgeting allows you to analyze the spending intelligently.

- Better financial decisions: Prioritizing investments and savings can inspire you to learn more about investing for the long term, which is crucial for creating a secure long-term plan.

Budgeting is the perfect strategy to help you avoid the quicksand of debt and financial instability, enabling you to focus on financial goals that lead to a stable future. You'll learn to set practical dreams within the possibilities of a budget that makes sense for you right now. Budgeting will make you economically disciplined. Budgeting ensures that you only spend on what you need and want, and not on what others want from you. It helps you to be prepared for that rainy day with savings as your emergency survival kit. Your budget informs you of what you can afford and what you can't afford (at least right now). It will enable you to focus on the value of the purchases you make, rather than on their packaging. It allows you to have all the information you need to plan your life strategically. Simply put, it puts you in charge.

## FINANCIAL PRINCIPLES

Two significant advantages that will result from 50/30/20 budgeting is that you can reduce debt over time and add to your investments. To understand how significant these advantages are, it is crucial to know the financial principles that guide debt and investment.

Long-term cost of debt: The cost of debt is a measure of the total interest that a person is paying on all of their obligations. To calculate the debt cost, the total of all interest paid yearly on debts is calculated and then divided by the total amount of the debt. This is the average interest paid on debts, and it shows debt results in loss over time. Why spend money on interest when it could be going toward your needs, wants, and savings?

Long-term value of investments: Investments are the other side of the coin because they accrue value over time, putting you in a better position in the long term. For that reason, it's important both to save and to invest.

As you regularly budget using the 50/30/20 plan, investing will become an opportunity for more financial education, including topics like these:

- How the stock markets work
- Evaluating company financial reports
- Studying business strategies and market forces
- Corporate leadership and ethics

## CHAPTER TWO

## THE 50/30/20 APPROACH TO BUDGETING

---

*"Balancing your money is the key to having enough." Elizabeth Warren*

At the beginning of this chapter, the quote addresses why budgeting and financial control are tied to happiness and why the 50/30/20 rule is so significant and relevant. The 50/30/20 rule involves budgeting and balancing one's money based on simple categorizations of **needs, wants, and savings**. These three categories represent everything that contends with your money. With so many potential decisions to make, having a plan like a 50/30/20 budget makes so

17

much sense if you plan to lead a fulfilling life and achieve your financial goals. This rule also helps you to manage your resources so that you will be able to lead a less stressful life.

The primary purpose of the 50/30/20 rule is to be able to adequately track your spending and take appropriate steps to allocate your income toward needs and wants while still making room for adequate savings. As a first step, you need to determine your monthly after-tax income, which is your income minus taxes, insurance, and other deductions. Once this is established, you can quickly assess and plan your budget within the 50/30/20 framework.

**Needs (50% of your income after tax):**

Needs are bills and expenses related to your essential survival—things like food, energy bills, housing, utilities, health insurance, transportation, child care, and minimum loan payments. A good rule of thumb is that your housing, rent, or mortgage payment should take no more than 30% of your entire income. Even if you are approved for a bigger loan where the cost is higher than 30% of your take-home pay, it's best to be conservative and not count on future raises to make up the difference. By holding down housing expenses, you have 20% left to spend on all of your other necessities.

**Wants (30% of your income after tax):**

The "30" in the 50/30/20 rule is dedicated to wants. Wants are discretionary items that we purchase just because we enjoy them, and they improve our lives. Wants can include any number of things like video and music streaming services, movies, gym memberships, vacations, and eating out. By allocating 30% of your income to something you want, you're able to enjoy your everyday life and spend on yourself without feeling guilty. But it's important to set a limit on this category because we all have an endless list of things we want and would like to do.

**Savings (20% of your income after tax):**

Saving should be an integral part of anyone's life. As a responsible person, it's essential to prepare for emergencies and retirement using savings and investments. Savings gives you the freedom to live your dreams, implement your ideas, and take advantage of investment opportunities. The 50/30/20 rule helps create a consistent and firm structure that allows you to make room for saving as well as paying off debt every month.

The rule helps to provide a bit of everything within your budget. So while setting aside funds for necessities and savings, the 50/30/20 rule also includes room for fun and enjoyment. Why not enjoy a good meal, take a vacation, and wear the clothes you like? Your balanced budget approach will take into account your current needs and wants without neglecting future needs.

## CHAPTER THREE

## HOW TO START BUDGETING

---

*"Budgeting is telling your money where to go instead of wondering where it went."* *John C. Maxwell.*

With financial management comes a certain degree of control over your own life, and budgeting is a vital part of that. Forget the myth that budgeting holds you back from a fulfilling life—it's actually the reverse. Budgeting just means that you want a lot more from life than just the basics and willing to expend some effort to achieve your goals. You might be wondering if this is going to involve a lot of bookkeeping and spreadsheets. It really doesn't have to, and you don't need extra training either. Budgeting is simply the ability to plan your money and direct where it goes instead of losing it without really knowing what happened. It means purposeful spending.

To do this, you need to do two basic things: 1) tracking your expenses, and 2) categorizing your expenses. This chapter goes through each of these and explains the concepts behind them thoroughly so that you can start budgeting right away.

**Set up your budget framework by calculating percentages for needs, wants, and savings according to the 50/30/20 rule**

After getting all the information required to implement the 50/20/30 rule, what's left is its actual calculation.

**Budget allocations example: Lindsay**

Lindsay earns an income of $5,000 per month after taxes, and other contributions have been deducted.

# 50/30/20 Budgeting

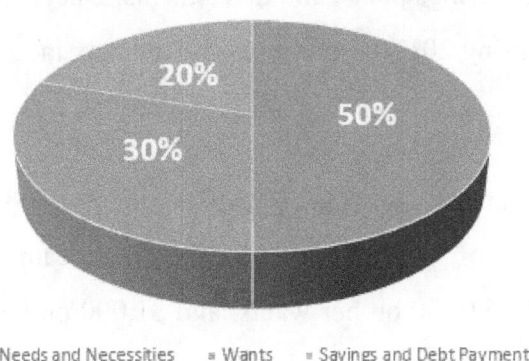

▪ Needs and Necessities    ▪ Wants    ▪ Savings and Debt Payment

## Needs

50% of $5,000= 50/100 × $5,000 =$2,500

This $2,500 will be used to cover expenses such as housing, clothing, food, and health, among others.

## Wants

30% of $5,000= 30/100 × $5,000 = $1,500

This $1,500 should be used toward wants, including things like traveling, entertainment, and eating out.

## Savings or debts

20% of $5,000= 20/100 × $5,000 = $1,000

This $1,000 should be allocated to emergency savings, employer savings plans, and investments. Debts can also be paid off using 20% of your monthly after-tax income.

To summarize, using the 50/30/20 model, Lindsay, who earns a pay of $5,000 after taxes, should allocate $2,500 on her needs, $1,500 on her wants, and $1,000 on her savings or debts.

**Tracking your expenses**

The next step toward your 50/30/20 budget is tracking your actual expenses. This will include all bills, debit, and credit transactions. Tracking your expenses is one of the primary tasks in the budget process. By monitoring your expenditures, you become more accountable to your financial future while having the ability to prioritize savings. Expense monitoring lets you track your financial progress, celebrate small wins, and appreciate those little steps you are taking toward achieving your set goals. Furthermore, monitoring expenses helps you identify shortcomings and know where to make necessary adjustments. This, in itself, keeps you motivated on your financial journey.

It is a lot better and easier to keep an orderly financial life than to sort out a messy one. When it comes to finances, there is no such thing as blissful ignorance. Tracking your expenses also helps you reduce impulsive spending, zero-in on wasteful spending, and know when to negotiate a better deal. This way, not only will you find it easier to save, you will be able to stay out of debt and remain focused on your financial journey.

## How to track your expenses

**Starting a budget**: Using the budget model and percentages in the previous section, you should be able to calculate your own personal budget with allocations for needs, wants, and savings.

**Listing your actual expenses by category:** This is one of the most crucial parts of this exercise. After putting your bills into categories, it's time to add in your debit and credit card transactions for the month. It is vital to record and document all of your actual expenses, including expected and unexpected expenses like car repairs, gifts, travel, eating out, veterinary bills, salon visits, shopping, and everything else.

25

**Monitor those numbers:** Do all these more incidental expenses put you over the limit for needs (50%) or wants (30%)? This part of the exercise is sure to provide some "Ah-ha!" moments. You might already be seeing places where your budget is out of alignment and where you can make some meaningful changes. This is an excellent opportunity to make adjustments, identify less expensive alternatives, or eliminate unnecessary or unimportant items.

**Nuts and bolts - How do you track your expenses?**

There are various ways to track your expenses. This chapter will discuss three methods. Since this will be an ongoing project, it's a good idea to dedicate time to set up the tools you'll need. Some alternative methods are:

**Paper and pencil method:** Set columns for needs, wants, and savings and put the limit you have calculated at the top of each column.  Then start listing your bills, debit, and credit charges in their proper columns. Total all three columns to see where it puts you in terms of total expense per category and category percentage. I advise keeping a notebook so that you can turn to a new page when a significant item changes and then recalculate where you stand.

**Spreadsheet method:** You do the same exercise in a spreadsheet, which has the advantage of automating the calculations. For this exercise, you can download a pre-formatted 50/30/20 Budget Spreadsheet. You can find information for downloading this file using the **link on page 7** of this book.

| 50 / 30 / 20 Budget | | | | | | | |
|---|---|---|---|---|---|---|---|

| Monthly sources of income | Sources | Monthly Amount | | | | | |
|---|---|---|---|---|---|---|---|
| | Source 1 | $ | 4,000.00 | | | | |
| | Source 2 | $ | - | | | | |
| | Source 3 | $ | - | | | | |
| | Source 4 | $ | - | | | | |
| *Total Take-home Income* | | $ | 4,000.00 | | | | |

| 50/30/20 Allocations | | Needs (50%) | | Wants (30%) | | Savings (20%) | |
|---|---|---|---|---|---|---|---|
| Total for category | | $ 2,000.00 | | $ 1,200.00 | | $ 800.00 | |
| List of Bills/and Expenditures | Housing | $ | - | Movies | $ - | 401k plan | $ - |
| (including credit/debit charges) | Food | $ | - | Gym membership | $ - | Emergency saving | $ - |
| | Insurance | $ | - | Subscriptions | $ - | Credit card 1 | $ - |
| | Car payment | $ | - | Sports | $ - | Credit card 2 | $ - |
| | Personal Care | $ | - | Hobbies | $ - | Loan 1 | $ - |
| | Basic clothing | $ | - | Vacations | $ - | Loan 1 | $ - |
| | Other | $ | - | Cable | $ - | | $ - |
| | Gas | $ | - | Wifi | $ - | | $ - |
| | Water | $ | - | Phone plan | $ - | | $ - |
| | Heat | $ | - | Phone | $ - | | $ - |
| | Eating out 1 | $ | - | Dry cleaning | $ - | | $ - |
| | Eating out 2 | $ | - | Car wash | $ - | | $ - |
| | Eating out 3 | $ | - | Gifts | $ - | | $ - |
| | Pet food | $ | - | Art | $ - | | $ - |
| | Veterinary bill | $ | - | Furniture | $ - | | $ - |
| | | $ | - | Books | $ - | | $ - |
| | | $ | - | Tickets | $ - | | $ - |
| | | $ | - | Jewelry | $ - | | $ - |
| | | $ | - | Clothing - extra | $ - | | $ - |
| | | $ | - | Entertaining | $ - | | $ - |
| | | $ | - | | $ - | | $ - |
| | | $ | - | | $ - | | $ - |
| Totals by category | | $ | - | | $ - | | $ - |
| Percentage of Total Take-home pay | | 0% | | 0% | | 0% | |

**Budgeting Apps:** You can also use a budgeting app on your phone or laptop. A budget application is always at hand and can make recording expenditures easier. Still, it may not be aligned with the 50/30/20 rule, so you might need to run the percentage calculations yourself.

Whichever method you use, the most important thing is to keep track of expenses and make progress toward your goals over time. There are several applications available on the App Stores.

**Categorizing your expenses**

While organizing your expenses, it is essential to keep things as simple as possible and track every payment.

Categorizing needs, wants, and savings:

- **Needs:** Be straightforward in your budget plan, but comprehensive. I recommend that your needs category include only these expenses:

  Housing: Money set aside to pay for shelter can include: mortgage payment, rent, household repairs, property taxes, renter's insurance, and HOA fees.

Transportation: Examples are taxis, bus passes, car payments, fuel, car repair, car insurance or warranty, tires, maintenance and oil changes, gas, parking fees, and registration and DMV fees.

Food: Groceries, meal tickets, eating out, food delivery fees, and pet food should all be recorded in needs.

Clothing: Clothing items for you, your spouse, and children, including shoes and outerwear, should be listed here.

Household supplies: Toiletries, dishwasher detergent, cleaning supplies, laundry detergent, tools, and so on all belong in this category.

Insurance: This would include anything you spend on health, life, homeowner's, or renter's insurance.

Personal Needs: Haircare, cosmetics, gym memberships, babysitters, prescriptions, and subscriptions should also be listed.

As you list all of your needs in this category, it's clear that you often have a lot of discretion over even your necessary purchases. Over time, even contracted items can be changed according to your plans.

## CHAPTER FOUR

## 50% - IDENTIFYING NEEDS AND OBLIGATIONS

---

*"If you know how to spend less than you get, you have the philosopher's stone." Benjamin Franklin*

Needs are simply the things that you cannot survive without physically, personally, or socio-economically. Expenditures like automobiles, mobile phones, and laptops can be considered needs or want depending on the circumstances. You may actually need a car, laptop, and phone to do your job. However, it's essential to differentiate the need aspect from the want aspect. Maybe you need a cell phone, but does it need to be a specific brand or carrier plan? Does the car need to be a particular size and brand? By carefully thinking

31

about how much control and discretion you have over the items you chose to buy, you can remove some of the pressure on your budget. This chapter helps you assess where you are and how you can bring your budget into alignment with the 50/30/20 rule.

## Assessing where you are and the steps needed to align with the 50/30/20 rule

Of all the categories of expenses, the needs are the most important. The level to which your needs are met directly affects your happiness and the quality of life.

Start by listing your needs and what you spent on them in the last month, including bills, debit, and credit payments. List needs and expenses in terms of importance under the headings on your budget tracker. By the end of this chapter, you will have gathered everything you need for budgeting according to the 50/30/20 rule.

**Prioritize your needs**: Prioritizing is the first and one of the most important steps toward an effective 50/30/20 rule of budgeting after need assessment. Once you have the data showing all your needs in detail, you can rank them. Generally speaking, you should be spending the most money on the most critical items.

**Set a 50% benchmark:** According to the 50/30/20 rule, 50% of your take-home pay should be dedicated to covering all of your needs. With the prioritized list and corresponding cost, you can establish a spending plan for essentials and prune some expenses (possibly on energy, groceries, or eating out) to align with the 50% spending limit.

# CHAPTER FIVE

## 30% - IDENTIFYING WANTS

---

*"Money looks better in the bank than on your feet."*
*Sophia Amoruso*

This 30% is all about balance. In theory, 30% for wants seems like plenty, but we have virtually unlimited wants in reality. That means that working with 30% will require assessing our own individual spending priorities. However, by limiting wants spending to 30% and knowing that we are adequately saving and paying down debts, we can fully enjoy what we buy purely for ourselves. Here is where the 50/30/20 rule shines because it allows you to maintain financial balance and achieve long-term goals while thoroughly enjoying your life today.

So what will you choose?

Spending on wants can include travel, vacations, eating out, entertainment, sports, cable TV, hair care, branded clothing, pets, hobbies, and décor. It's up to you whether you'd like to improve your home, spend money with your friends, or spend it on yourself. When making these decisions, it's essential to realize that you have a lot of control over when, how, and how much you spend. You can also change your choices and priorities at any time. Keeping the 50/30/20 rule in mind will help you make better decisions that benefit you in the long term.

Decision-making perspective

This diagram can put things in perspective by helping us decide how and when to spend our cash. Let's take a look.

## THE DECISON GRID DIAGRAM

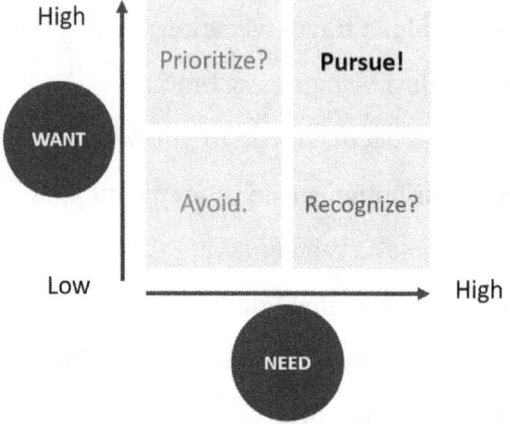

**Low wants and low needs**: According to the diagram, if something is low on the want scale and the need scale, we should just AVOID it.

**Low wants and high needs**: Sometimes, we need something but would rather not spend the money. This grid suggests that we RECOGNIZE AND PRIORITIZE that expense.

**High wants and low needs:** This is the hardest one to deal with. When we really want something, it's pretty easy to convince ourselves that we need it, even it sends our spending off the rails. The grid recommends AVOID as the best strategy. As a practical matter, I think delaying can also be a reliable tactic. Over time, savings and sales might create a situation where it fits into the budget.

**High wants and high needs:** This one is an easy decision. We just PRIORITIZE and PURSUE.

## Keeping up with the Joneses versus setting your path

You've probably heard of "keeping up with the Joneses." Its modern equivalent is perhaps "leading an Instagram-worthy life." What does that have to do with keeping and saving money? Should Instagram and the "Joneses" really have much influence over our spending? By staying in touch with your own financial reality and your own values, you can minimize some of that pressure.

## Setting your own path.

**Be sure of your values:** Aligning your values with your habits is the key to more fulfillment. Establishing and reinforcing your beliefs and values keep you from getting carried away by what others do and whatever image they are projecting. That way, you won't throw away money on things that you don't really believe in and don't fulfill a desire you actually have. It's OK to admire and congratulate, but don't necessarily buy into what everyone else is doing. Follow your own path.

**Plan for things that make you happy:** It's one of life's pure pleasures to know you have enough of what you need. It's even better when you feel you can afford some of the things you want. Part of the experience that budgeting brings is the pleasure of planning toward some memorable and rewarding experiences, whether, for you, that means travel, the home of your dreams, or something else entirely. With a 50/30/20 budget, you're definitely planning to have the things you want as well as the things you need.

**A company of like-minded friends**: If "keeping up with the Joneses" hit home because you are surrounded by neighbors, friends, and work friends where spending is a fierce competition, maybe it's time to branch out. You deserve family and friends that support your goals and dreams. With financial discipline, you really can have it all.

## CHAPTER SIX

## 20% - SAVINGS AND INVESTMENTS

---

*"Look everywhere to cut a little bit from your expenses. It will add up to a significant sum." Suze Orman*

The 50/30/20 rule advocates for 20% of your monthly income going to savings and/or debt reduction. There are several reasons that savings are essential, and they include:

**Planning for the unexpected:**

You can't predict the experiences you will have in life; what you can do is plan to be ready. Life happens, sometimes positively, other times not so much, and an unexpected event can put a dent in your finances. Preparing for the unexpected falls into three main categories:

**Emergency fund:** We all know the stress of unexpected bills. Ideally, an emergency fund should cover about six months of your living expenses. You can build an emergency fund over time by including it in your monthly budget in the 20% category.

**Insurance:** Insurance can reduce risk by protecting critical things such as your life, health, vehicle, house, and household goods. By having enough insurance, you can protect yourself from some emergency expenses.

**Big plans - Retirement, owning a home, education, and vacations**. Putting in place a five-, ten-, or twenty-year plan can help you be more consistent and visionary when it comes to your future aspirations and goals. Once you've put your emergency fund in place, it's time to start putting money away in investments. Understanding risk, reward, and your best investment options will make it much more likely that you'll achieve your long-term plans and desires.

**Methods of saving:**

**Your company 401k savings plan:**

If your company offers a tax-deferred savings plan, this is an excellent way to get started on saving for the future. It has the advantage of putting aside money automatically and regularly. Importantly, it will be either a tax-deferred plan where you pay taxes when you withdraw money after retirement, or it will be a Roth plan where you pay taxes now but owe no taxes later.

If your company offers a matching contribution, it's an even better deal, and you might be able to achieve 10% savings very easily. Then you will be halfway to following the 50/30/20 rule for savings. If you cannot put in a large percentage when you start a 401k plan right now, I recommend upping your contribution by 1-2% whenever you get a raise. That way, you will have more money going into savings and more money for wants and needs.

**Stocks:** Stocks are shares in a particular company, which equates to owning a fraction of the company. Stockholders may be entitled to dividends as the company grows and makes a profit annually or quarterly. Historically, stocks have outperformed many other forms of investment over time. A stock's value appreciates for companies that grow and are more successful. There are many good books for beginning investors that explain how to evaluate and purchase stocks.

**Savings accounts:** Savings accounts are the way to start saving, although once you have established your emergency fund, it's time to move on to higher-yielding investments. Your emergency fund savings account should be in a secure bank or credit union and entirely insured by the FDIC. Balancing cash on hand against investment is vital so that your assets can grow over time.

**Checking accounts:** Your checking account should also be at a healthy balance to avoid unnecessary overdraft charges. Your emergency fund should not be kept in your checking account but in a separate account that is only used for actual emergencies. It should not be viewed as a splurging account.

**Acorns and other spare change applications:** The Acorns app is a new way to set aside spare change. In effect, it's a lot like throwing your spare change in a jar and depositing it in the bank later. The Acorns app works by rounding up purchases to the nearest dollar and depositing that amount into an investment plan. For students, Acorns is free, but others pay a monthly fee until they reach $5,000. An app like this may not make sense on tiny balances because the fees are high; however, it benefits from being automatic. You might want to try something like this as a supplement to a more intentional strategy.

# CHAPTER SEVEN

# CONCLUSION

---

*"The art is not making money, but keeping it."*
*Anonymous*

### Setting your intentions

When it comes to being financially secure, intentions are one of the most important things to consider because it really is a marathon. Building your wealth is a journey that takes a lot of time—even your entire life. Set out your goals and draw the pathway to achieving them. This way, your steps will consistently shape your habits, which will, in turn, lead to a healthy financial lifestyle. You can even set monthly, yearly, and longer-term goals.

Will intentions be enough? Maybe not. So, how else can you build reinforcements around your goals, dreams, and choices?

Here are some ways that will help you stick to your 50/30/20 budget plan:

- Envision the things and lifestyle that you want

- Draw up a comprehensive budget for this year, as well as one for next year

- Continue to adhere to a 50/30/20 budget.

- Surround yourself with good friends who understand and share your goals

- Take a step, make a change, and commit to yourself.

- Share your new plan with friends and family and get their support.

- Post quotes around your house where you can see your goals every day.

- Keep a journal of progress and new ideas as well as hopes and dreams.

- Gather support from family and your partner or spouse.

Now that you fully understand the 50/30/20 budget rule and how it can help you organize and prioritize your finances, you just need to get going. It's one of the most straightforward approaches you will find, easy to implement, and surely will lead to a more balanced approach to your finances.

## More

---

If you enjoyed this book or found it useful, I'd be very grateful if you'd post a short review on Amazon. Your support really does make a difference, and I read all the reviews personally so I can get your feedback.

***Thanks again for your support!***